AWESOME THINGS YOU MUST DO IN RETIREMENT

ULTIMATE GUIDE TO AN AWESOME LIFE AFTER WORK

JAMES HALL

Information contained within this book is for educational purpose only. Although the author and publisher have made every effort to ensure that the information in this book was correct at press time, the author and publisher do not assume and hereby disclaim any liability to any party for any loss, damage, or disruption caused by errors or omissions, whether such errors or omissions result from negligence, accident, or any other cause.

Table of Contents

FOREWORD

WHAT DO YOU THINK OF when you hear the word '**retirement**'? Do you think of boredom or do you feel your stomach turn into a double knot? Well, I am here to inform you that you have absolutely nothing to fear. You have everything to gain. Boredom? I don't think so. Gone are days of retirement being the dreaded last chapter of your life. Retirement is anything but a period in your life where you begin to slowly lose your own identity and drift off into the abyss. Retirement is what you make it!

Yes, it is true you are going to have quite a bit of new-found time on your hands, and if you don't fill it with something meaningful or that you enjoy---of course you'll be bored! There are so many different things out there in the world you have the freedom to pursue. The only question is what you will decide to do?

So, what will you decide to do? What are they, exactly? What is on your list? There are so many awesome possibilities out there. How many things you should do in your retirement? Is it 99 things? Or is it 101? Nope. There are many more than that. You're retired, and nothing should hold you back. The sky is the limit, so get out there and have fun.

"You are never too old to set a new goal or dream a new dream."-C.S. Lewis

In this book you will find your ultimate specific suggestions, ideas, and things to inspire you to make this chapter the greatest chapter of your life.

How many awesome things that are listed in this book? I do not know. I lost track. But I know for sure it's more than 99, or 101 things that other books out there are listing just to fill the pages. If you have time, I'd challenge you to count how many to-do things in this book. But I doubt you will have any time, because after reading this book, I'm sure you will be super busy fulfilling your awesome retirement life.

CHAPTER 1: Seeing the World – Nature and Animals

YOU HAVE WORKED 30-40+ YEARS, perhaps you've paid off your house or student loans for your kids. You have definitely put in your time. Now it's time for you to have the freedom to do what you want to do. Before you jump right into the deep end of the retirement pool, you should make sure you know your complete financial situation. How much are able to spend while maintaining your current lifestyle? How much will you need to spend to get where you want to be?

You don't want to go on a month long safari in Africa or purchase a villa in Tuscany without having a complete understanding of your finances.

You are someone who loves more dogs or cats than you do people! You count your pet as one of your best friends. You love going to the zoo and seeing all the exotic animals. Your big dream is to one day see the African bushland.

Here are ideas that are bound to get your approval. If you are an animal or nature lover, these ones are for you!

* * *

Start a small pet sitting business

There are many facilities for dogs and cats but very few for hamsters or miniature pot-bellied pigs. Look into your local and state regulations to see what's required for you to start a pet sitting business.

* * *

Start a "U-Pick" flower garden

People pick and create their own flower bouquets and arrangements. You can charge them per flower or per floral arrangement. Get creative and make sure there's enough variety with the flowers you choose to grow.

* * *

Move to a tropical island

Sell all your possessions and bid your friends and family goodbye. You will send a postcard once you're settled in paradise.

* * *

Become a florist

Do you love flowers? Are you creative? Discover how to become a florist. Spread the word and advertise your services over social media.

* * *

Become a Survivalist

Move to Alaska. Alaska is an incredible place to live. It has breathtaking views of the stars at night. It has immense amounts of wildlife. It also has tax breaks for those that live there. The average wage is also much higher than the average wage in the continental United States.

* * *

Invest in property

Beach front or potential property that might be the next commercial shopping district. There are many opportunities out there and lots of good steals—you just have to know where to look. It's best to find a buyers' agent to steer you in the right direction.

* * *

Set up bird feeders

Depending on how large of a property you have to work with and climate will determine how many you should set up. Set up bird feeders and different heights and use different food. Make one feeder with a sugar solution that attracts hummingbirds. Set up a motion sensor camera to record the action at some of the feeders or just pull up a chair and get a pair of binoculars. Having a bird book on hand to look up the different types of birds you will see might also come in handy.

* * *

Foster a pregnant cat or dog

The animal rescue organization or shelter will generally provide food and pet supplies in return for you providing a safe, warm, quiet place for the mother cat or dog to give birth to her babies. When the kittens or puppies are around 8 weeks old they will probably be placed up for adoption as will the mother cat. You should get first dibs if you would like to adopt but at the very least you will be able to meet the potential adopters and decide if they are suitable or not—which will be reassuring.

* * *

Plan a trip to the great state of Texas

Howdy, partner! Yes, Texas! There is so much to do in Texas. It's an amazing state with so many different types of terrain and climate. From the Houston Space Center to the larger-than-life TEXAS the musical. It's a state you could spend months in and not see everything there is to see. Instead of staying at a chain hotel or motel, why not really try and immerse yourself in the culture of Texas by staying at one of the highly rated bed & breakfasts? Hosts of bed & breakfasts are usually very talkative and love giving advice or providing invaluable information to tourists. You'll get the inside scoop!

Visit the Grand Canyon

Millions of years of geographical history will be right before your eyes. There are many guided tours offered throughout the area. You can take an overnight camping adventure or just a day trip hiking the park.

* * *

Raise chickens

Sell the eggs. Chickens are relatively low maintenance and easy to raise. You need a chicken coop, fencing, and depending on what part of the country you live in—a heater.

* * *

Live off the land

Grow your own food and make your own clothes. Give yourself a year to really immerse yourself in this new way of life. If Laura Ingalls Wilder could do it with her Ma and Pa why can't you?!

* * *

Sell your house

Buy a house boat. Get rid of the house that is tying you down to one location. Purchase a house boat and get to tour and see a different sight every single day. Travel up and down the Mississippi River. Sail around the coast of Florida.

* * *

Make dog collars and/or leashes

Donate them to a local animal shelter or sell them and donate a percentage of the proceeds to an animal related charitable organization.

* * *

Volunteer at an animal shelter

Animal shelters run on tight budgets and are always looking for volunteers to socialize with the animals, walk dogs, or clean cages.

* * *

South America

Africa seems to be one of those countries that's on quite a few bucket lists—and it's easy to understand why. Exotic animals in a majestic foreign landscape but why not travel to South America? Go and see Afica but don't forget about South America. The wildlife and beauty found in parts of South America are equally as wondrous as Africa.

* * *

Nature photographer

Focus on a specific niche like birds or waterfalls. You can travel the state finding interesting subjects or travel the country! You can turn your photographs into beautiful calendars or canvas art work.

On a clear night sleep under the moon and stars. Bring a telescope. Leave the cellphone and other technology in the house.

* * *

Visit every waterfall in your state

Go to your state's national park website and look up all the different waterfalls. Check out local guidebooks to find any obscure waterfall that might only be known to a very, very small local population—they do exist and when you find them it feels like you've stumbled on gold at the end of a rainbow! Magical!

* * *

Visit every national park in the United States

There are 58 national parks in the United States. Yellowstone, the Grand Canyon, and Yosemite are just a couple parks in our incredible national park system.

Do you remember reading *Around the World in 80 Days* by Jules Verne in school? Well why not really go around the world on a world cruise? Holland American, Cunard, and Pavlus all offer many different world cruise packages. Anywhere from 89 to 145 nights. It's a cost-effective way to get to see and experience many different parts of the world! China, Italy, Australia, Norway—you name it, you can go there! Go to sleep in Hawaii and wake up in Fiji!

Visit Montana and learn how to fly-fish. Fly-fishing is where you use an artificial fly to catch real fish. This is usually done in lakes, rivers, and streams. Visit a Cabelas or other outdoor sports store to get more information and talk to professional fly-fishermen. Even better would be to sign up for a class or take a fly-fishing vacation.

* * *

Start a community vegetable garden

Find some public and/or common ground for everyone to plant something and everyone that plants something can share with everyone else. It's a great way to obtain, at very minimal cost, crisp and delicious vegetables. To spread the word pass out flyers door-to-door in your neighborhood or apartment building.

* * *

Visit Alaska either by land or cruise ship

There are many tour agencies available but you could also just do your own due diligence and put together your own dream itinerary. Would you like to see a polar bear up close and personal or take a walk on an iceberg? Go do it—what are you waiting for?

***

Bring your dog or cat to visit residents in a nursing hom

Most residents love being able to pet a dog or cat. It might bring back wonderful childhood memories of when they had their own pets. Make sure to check with the proper nursing home officials before showing up. Some nursing homes have policies against animals that aren't service animals on the premises.

***

Cross the Atlantic Ocean by ship

Cunard and Royal Caribbean are two ship lines that offer Trans-Atlantic cruise itineraries. 7-day to 43-day packages are available depending on the time of year you wish to take the trip.

***

Walk around the North island of New Zealand

Take a guided tour of Hobbiton, the actual 'Middle-Earth' from the *The Lord of the Rings* trilogy. This land is magnificent and its beauty is astoundingly breathtaking. It will make you cry it's so magnificent. For lunch and dinner there is even a Shire's Rest Café. You will be awed by the green, lush rolling hills even if you have never picked up any of J.R.R. Tolkien's books.

* * *

Take an African safari

Africa is a dream destination for many people. It's not hard to understand why! There are an unforgettable number of exotic animals that you have only been able to see in a zoo. The sights and scenery are out-of-this-world extraordinary. Look up and do your research on reputable travel agencies that specialize in African safaris. Don't be afraid to go. This is one vacation you will never regret taking or forget.

* * *

Happy Easter! Enjoy and experience Easter in Saint Peter's Basilica

Even if you are not Roman Catholic visiting the Vatican and Saint Peter's Basilica is a phenomenal, surreal experience. Going any time is magnificent but going during Easter is just a little extra magical. The Pope will give a service lasting a little under 2 hours. If you go during Christmas or Easter you will need to apply for tickets. The earlier you apply for tickets the better chances you have of getting them. During the summer months the Pope also gives a service in Saint Peter's Square. He will come out on the balcony and bless the entire audience. Summers are usually very hot and they only have so many seats available. Show up early to get a seat and make sure to bring plenty of water and sunscreen.

CHAPTER 2: Music Makes the World Go Round

IS MUSIC IN YOUR HEART AND SOUL? Do you feel more alive when you listen to music? If you answered yes, (and who doesn't), then you will definitely enjoy one of these fun carefully curated selections. These have been chosen with someone like you in mind.

Attend an opera

You might be surprised to find out that you actually enjoy Mozart. *Figaro's Wedding* is one of the most popular operas of all-time.

***

Learn to play a musical instrument

If you already know how to play the piano and acoustic guitar, why not try something a little different like a xylophone or a ukulele?

***

Become a groupie!

Who is your favorite music artist or group? Plan your next vacation around their tour dates. Even in their 80s the Rolling Stones still actively tour.

***

Go to as many Broadway shows as you can!

Les Miserables, Cats, and *Phantom of the Opera* are just a few of some of the incredible shows you can find on Broadway.

***

Take a trip to Las Vegas

That's right, Sin City. Contrary to popular belief you do not need to spend all your money at the casinos. You can have an incredible time not visiting a single casino! Crazy, isn't it? There are hundreds of performances---comedy shows, *Cirque du Soleil,* and popular artists. Pay a visit to the infamous Mob Museum or take a hike through Red Rock Canyon.

* * *

Joining a local music group or band

Did you play an instrument in high school or college? Do you love music? Joining a local music group or band might be the perfect creative outlet for you. Look for flyers at coffee houses or music venues. You could also post in online community forums—that you are seeking a music group or band in need of a guitar player? Vocalist? Drummer? Hey the *Rolling Stones* are in their 70s and still rocking it out—and they have no signs of slowing down anytime soon!

CHAPTER 3: Get Your Creative Juices Flowing

BEING CREATIVE IS IN YOUR BLOOD. You love creating things and learning new ideas and concepts. You see the world with a glass half-full attitude and that kind of attitude will only serve you well in the future! Here are ideas that will get your creative juices flowing and make you excited about retirement:

***

Create a comic book series

Create a comic book series either in-print or online. There are thousands of templates available online and many great prompts to get your creative juices spinning.

* * *

Record your life history

Record your life history either in a book or by video. Get a friend or family member to interview you, asking you questions about your life.

* * *

Create your family tree

You can join a website like Ancestry.com or Genealogybank.com and trace your roots. Did your great-great-great-great grandparents come over on the Mayflower? Are you related to Winston Churchill or President Andrew Jackson? You might be surprised what you find!

Scan and document all those old family photos you have stuffed away in boxes. Later on you can create a slideshow or film.

* * *

Learn a new language

Once you've mastered the language treat yourself to a trip to that region or country. Rosetta Stone is a language program that allows you to learn from the comfort of your own home. It's been around since 1996 and offers 28 different language packs.

* * *

Start a blog

What are you interested in? You could start visiting restaurants and blogging about your experiences/reviewing the service and food or perhaps you want to share funny stories and pictures of your grandkids. Let your imagination run wild!

* * *

Become an expert in a unique subject matter

Some ideas include: Checkers, Indian cooking,

astronomy, Faberge eggs, and miniature ponies. You will definitely not be lacking for any ice breakers at your next cocktail party.

***

Write your autobiography

Everyone has a story to tell, why not tell yours?

***

Take poetry classes

Take poetry classes (unless you already know a great deal about poetry) and teach what you learn to children in needy and/or inner-city areas. Poetry is a wonderful way to get children to learn how to express themselves through words.

***

Teach English as a second language

You can do this at your local library or even sign up with an organization that sends volunteers overseas to teach in third world countries. It's a great opportunity to see different parts of the world while providing a tremendous service for someone else.

* * *

Take classes at a community college or university

Many higher educational institutions provide low-cost or free options for non-credit seeking students. There aren't just Math and English classes there are often classes on local history, genealogy, or other interesting subjects.

* * *

Learn how to make soap and/or candle

It's a very fun hobby and you can sell your products at local craft fairs on Etsy, the largest and most popular craft website. Take a look around Etsy and see what people are interested in and buying. There is so much talent out there! Be inspired.

* * *

Design T-Shirts

Join a website like Teespring.com or Cafepress.com. You can come up with your own apparel and accessory designs. Think of some funny or inspirational sayings and put them on products. The great thing about this is you don't need any inventory or have any start-up costs. You get paid when your items sell. The website takes a certain percentage of your sales---the percentage depends on what site you choose to make and sell your designs on. You can advertise thru word of mouth or invest in some social media advertisements like Facebook ads.

* * *

Become a film critic

Do you like watching movies? Can you utter every line in *Casablanca* or *The Godfather?* Start with a small publication or newsletter and expand fom there.

* * *

Calling all artists

Open up a fun, upbeat art studio. People of all ages are welcome to come and paint. You can host birthday parties, bridal showers, school field trips, and so much more. This is such a wonderful alternative to having the same old event in a boring conference room or pizza place. This would take a bit of investment but one you could recoup by charging appropriately for time in the studio. Painting supplies, utilities, rent would all need to be covered. Publicity and promotion could be done with little to no money. With social media and word-of-mouth at your disposal paying an arm and leg for radio or print ads is unnecessary.

* * *

Etsy

Are you crafty? Do you make your own candles or knit your own blankets? If so, you can open up an Etsy shop. Etsy is a person-to-person e-commerce website made up of handmade or vintage goods. Etsy is a great community of talented entrepreneurs!

* * *

Looking for an Encore Career

The 'encore' career. You have already had a very successful career in whatever industry you are in but you are looking to get something more out of life. You know there is something else out there for you but you're just not sure what. Maybe you want more control over your finances and not have a 'big brother' hovering over you or perhaps you just want a career that makes you inspired and excited?

More and more people that are entering retirement are seeking an 'encore' career. It is definitely not unusual. These are some examples that people have transitioned into and really had good success with:

* * *

Get involved in public service

Run for public office. Have you ever wanted to be

mayor? Maybe not—but maybe you've thought of being on the board of something? School board?

* * *

Become a professional inn-sitter/innkeeper

Owners of bed & breakfasts work 24/7, 7 days a week. On the rare occasion they are able to get away, they need to find someone they can trust to take care of their guests. There are many agencies that you can sign up with or you could even start your own inn-sitting business. It would be a great way to see different parts of the country.

Open a bed and breakfast

Opening up a B&B isn't a decision that should be taken lightly. You will be tied to your business every single day unless you hire a property manager or someone to oversee the day-to-day operations of the business.

Create hair bows and barrettes

There are tutorials easily available online as well as in bookstores. Sell them at craft fairs.

Take a class to become a volunteer first responder

Classes are usually offered by a local educational institution, police department, or hospital.

Become a grant writer

Do you like writing? Become a grant writer for a non-profit organization or a freelance grant writer, accepting short-term assignments.

* * *

Work from home as a virtual assistant

There are many sources to find more information on what exactly being a virtual assistant entails but generally it involves organization email, updating calendars, and typing up documents or spreadsheets. You should have good overall knowledge of computers.

* * *

Write for The Richest or Buzzfeed

The applications are not too lengthy and they're usually accepted on a rolling basis. If you like reading tabloid news or writing lists about things that are entertaining—this could be a fun opportunity for you.

* * *

Become a Private Investigator

Do you like detective work? You could be a private investigator. Find missing people, go after deadbeat parents for failing to pay child support, trail potentially unfaithful spouses. You could be a real life Nancy Drew or Hardy boy.

* * *

Teach a class at a community college

Do you have years of experience in a certain field/or industry? Offer to teach a course. Some community colleges offer classes for foreign students that teach life skills or American culture.

* * *

Freelance Editor

Do you enjoy writing or editing papers? Sign up for a free profile on a website such as Upwork, which is a freelance website, and offer your services. When you first start, set a pay rate that's on the low-end so that you can gain some credibility and reviews. When you receive some good reviews then it's time to consider increasing your pay rate. Make sure to check out the ratings of your potential clients too—you want to make sure they have an excellent track record—easy to work and communicate with, reasonable expectations, and trustworthy.

* * *

The Dog Whisperer

Do you have a talent for training or teaching dogs? Why not take a course at a community college or online university to become a certified dog trainer? Now you don't have to have a certification to offer your services training dogs but it wouldn't hurt to have some education backing your training techniques and it would build clients trust in you.

*** *

Open up a comic book shop

With the resurgence of popular superhero movies like *Spiderman* and *Dark Knight*, comic books are coming back into the spotlight. Do you have a stash of your old childhood comic books in the basement or in the back of a closet collecting dust? Well now is your chance to dust them off and let them see the light of day. You don't need to have a physical store. You can sell on eBay or Amazon.

*** *

Rental Property

Do you live in a popular tourist destination? Do you live near a college or university? If you have a large home with extra bedrooms, you could rent out a room during the tourist season or for the school year.

***

Mary Poppins

Do you enjoy children? Are you in need of some extra income? Why not be a nanny. Depending on your specific life circumstances you can be a live-in nanny for someone or live-out and in your own home. You can work part-time or full-time. There are various websites that allow potential nannies to register and they can match you up with someone that is looking for your specific skillset. It would be beneficial to have already taken an early education course or at the bare minimum a pediatric CPR/First Aid course.

***

Missionary

Do you belong to a church? Check out any upcoming missionary trips. If there aren't any at your church, look around at other churches of the same denomination. You can be a missionary within the continental United States or travel abroad. They vary in length, from a few weeks to a year or more. Spread the word of the Lord and experience an entirely different culture while doing it. It's something that's life-changing not only for you but for those you come into contact with too!

Find Fido

Be a pet detective. Find lost pets. People post signs and contact information in the newspapers every day for pets that have gone missing. Use your P.I. skills and get to work. "Alrrrrighty then." (Yes, that's an Ace Ventura reference.)

Sports Writer

Become a sports columnist for a local newspaper. This would be excellent for the sports enthusiast that loves just about any and all sports, especially high school and college level as that's what most local papers cover 80% of the time. Start by writing your own online blog and getting a few solid pieces on there. When you feel the time is right, submit them to your local paper. They might want you to cover the local sports online and will link to your blog or they may take a chance and put you directly in print. Although rare, it does happen.

* * *

Tour Guide

Museum tour guide. Do you have a favorite museum in your area or are you passionate about history, utomobiles, or art? If so, you might try applying to be a tour guide. Depending on the museum this could either be a paid or volunteer position. The great thing about being a volunteer is that although you won't get monetary compensation you might get some great seats or tickets for all the museum's events!

* * *

Online Investing

Online investment opportunities are everywhere. Buying and selling websites is big business. You will need to have a pretty good grasp of technology or a willingness to learn in order to make a decent amount of money. Do you have knowledge of SEO or web analytics? If so, web site investments might be right up your alley!

* * *

Gender Reveal Custom Cakes

Make custom gender cakes for mothers or parents-to-be. Instead of the ultrasound technician telling the parents the gender of the baby, the technician will either tell you on the telephone or give a note to the parents to present to you and the gender will be written on the note. You will then either make a pink or blue cake or frost it in white or chocolate frosting. Then, at a party or family get together the cake is cut in front of everyone revealing the new baby's gender.

* * *

Drivers Ed Instructor

You have many years of driving under your belt. At some DMV locations they hire experienced drivers with good driving records to be drivers ed instructors and to administer driving tests. There are also private companies that offer drivers tests as well that could be looking for people. This is a job you must definitely be level-headed, brave, and very quick to take action (e.g. your student misses a stop sign and there's an oncoming vehicle).

* * *

Direct Sales

Join a direct sales company. Direct sales involves selling a product and recruiting others to sell product. They're also known as MLMs or multi-level marketing businesses. People either like the idea or hate it, there's really no in-between. Some of the more popular, established companies include: Tupperware, PartyLite, Avon, Mary Kay, and Discovery Toys. Other MLMs that have only been in the game a few years but seem to be on an upward growth trajectory include: Scentsy, Arbonne, Usborne Books and More, and Thirty-One Gifts. Find a sponsor that you can relate to and get along with. Ask lots and lots of questions before signing. Are there any monthly minimums to remain an active consultant? Is my area oversaturated? What are your average weekly sales?

Do you have a knack for wrapping gifts? Do people always compliment the way you wrap a present? Put together gift baskets and wrap gifts during the holidays. Charge a set fee per package. You could set up a booth during a craft fair or at a shopping mall.

Fraternity Cook

Are you an amazing cook? Do you live near a college or university campus? If so, put up flyers offering healthy, home-cooked meals to sororities and fraternities. Some Greek houses will even put out ads seeking cooks—check campus classified advertisements.

* * *

Interior Design Consultation

Do you have an eye for design or interior décor? Why not start your own interior design consultation business?

* * *

Professional Home Stager

Become a professional home stager. Many homeowners and real estate agents higher professional home stagers to come in and make the property more appealing to potential buyers. You would probably find more clients in a higher population area.

* * *

Genealogist

Everyone at some point or another thinks to themselves, "Where did I come from?". There are many people out there that would love to learn about their roots and heritage. They want to track down their great-great-great grandparents or other missing relatives. If you love genealogy, research, and reading-you might be able to help connect these people with vital pieces of information.

Become a member of Ancestry.com or GenealogyBank.com and start exploring your own family tree. Take some of the free tutorials and learn all the tips and tricks you can. Begin asking friends and family if they need help finding anyone or want to know where they come from. When you have a bit of experience and success, then it's time to start charging for your services. You can advertise your services at university archival centers, Craigslist, or online genealogy community forums. It's an incredible feeling to be able to track down someone's missing great-great grandmother or find a copy of a handwritten World War II registration for someone's father. After your first successful 'find' you'll be hooked!

* * *

Baker

Are you constantly being asked to bake and

decorate birthday, anniversary, or even wedding cakes for friends and family? Why not turn your talent into an opportunity to earn a little bit of extra cash? You can start by using word-of-mouth advertising. Spread the word to your family, friends, and those who you have done cakes for in the past that you are starting a new business venture and are going to be looking for new clients.

* * *

Life Coach

Do people come to you for advice or guidance? You could start a new career as a life coach. Help people refine their goals and learn how to focus and accomplish their dreams. It would be an extremely flexible opportunity to help someone and give back. You could work with only a certain age demographic like college students or all ages---it would be your business so completely up to you. You've already had success in one profession or industry why not help someone else achieve the same success?

* * *

Commercial Truck Driver

Obtain your CDL. Learn to drive commercial trucks. You'll get to see parts of the country not many people ever get to see. This would be a great encore career for someone that enjoys driving, isn't attached or stuck in one location, loves being independent, and thrives spending time alone.

* * *

Online Foreign Language Instructor

Are you proficient in a foreign language? Teach a class online. You can also create a series of videos or podcasts.

* * *

Realtor

Become a real estate agent. You have decades of business experience and have made many connections. It's time to put your connections to good use. Get in touch with them by being completely real and authentic.

CHAPTER 4: Ready for a Challenge?

ARE YOU LOOKING FOR SOMETHING EXHILARATING? Do you want to do something that takes a tremendous amount of strength, stamina, or will-power? If you're ready for a challenge, so are we! Take a look and see if you get inspired to pursue greatness:

***

Swim across the English Channel

Swim across a lake, canal, or if you're really up for a challenge—the English Channel. In 2014, 70-

year old Cyril Baldock swam the English Channel, a distance of 21.1 miles! A pretty incredible feat for any person let alone someone that's 70-years old! Isn't that amazing? Age shouldn't be a limiting factor in achieving your goals and dreams.

* * *

P90X

Start a new exercise routine. P90X or TurboFire are both workouts that can be done in the comfort of your own home using at-home workout DVDs. You don't need too much space but you do need an area free of clutter or anything you might hit yourself against.

* * *

Rock Climbing

Learn how to rock climb. Start by taking classes at a local gym or perhaps you have a rock climbing facility near you. It's a fun hobby that requires strength and agility. You don't have to start out climbing Mount Kilimanjaro you can completely enjoy just climbing around the gym's rock climbing wall. It's an excellent work out!

* * *

Run a marathon

Train and run a marathon. This is not something you can just sign up for and run the next day. A marathon is 26.2 grueling miles. It takes a lot of physical and mental preparation and strength. If you don't think a marathon is something you would want to do, try a half-marathon or even a 10K. The preparation involved could take a year or longer but if you have the drive, ambition, and willingness to set a goal—this is already a set ahead the majority of the population.

* * *

Run for a Cause

Go for a run or walk and raise money for a cause. Watch the documentary of the Canadian athlete and cancer activist, Terry Fox, and get inspired. Terry Fox was an incredible young man who died at the young age of 22. He raised millions of dollars running across Canada before cancer overtook and spread throughout his body forcing him to quit. The Terry Fox Foundation has raised over $650 million dollars for cancer research since its inception in 1988.If you have always been afraid of heights, you can push past your fears and take a leap of faith!

* * *

Sky-Diving

Sky-diving is something many have on their bucket lists but few will actually do! If it's on your bucket list—just do it! There's no better feeling that pushing past and conquering a fear.

* * *

Break a World Record

Break a world record. What world record? That's up to you. Purchase the latest edition of Guinness and find a record you'd like to try and break. What will it be—pie eating? Growing the largest pumpkin? Growing the longest pinky fingernail? Remembering the most numbers of Pi (3.14...)? Have some fun picking something to break!

CHAPTER 5: Volunteer Opportunities

DO YOU WANT TO LEAVE A LASTING LEGACY in this world? Are you hoping to make a positive impact on someone's life? There are some amazing opportunities available for you to accomplish both of these things.

* * *

Visit nursing homes and teach the residents how to paint

Most nursing homes have community recreation directors or organizers. Get in touch with them and offer your services. Let them know what hours you are available and how many people you would feel comfortable instructing at a time.

* * *

Lend a hand at a hospice center

Hospice centers are often short-staffed and are appreciative of volunteers to come during the breakfast, lunch, or dinner hours to help feed residents.

* * *

Crochet or Knit

Crochet or knit slippers and mittens. Donate them or give them as gifts to friends and family.

* * *

Medical transport driver

Volunteer as a medical transport driver for Little Brothers Friends of the Elderly. Elders that have no way of getting to and from important doctor appointments due to an extremely limited income are able to contact Little Brothers and Little Brothers matches them up with a driver. Be prepared to wait awhile while they're in their appointment—you just never know how long the appointments will take.

***

Donate to a women's shelter

Collect travel sized or sample sized personal hygiene products and toiletries. Donate them to an abused women's shelter.

***

Bring toiletries to the needy people in your town

Are there people living on street corners or near underpasses? Many homeless people don't have access to personal hygiene products. Things like soap, hand sanitizer, deodorant, and toothpaste are considered luxury items. Ask stores or neighbors/friends for donations of these items or money to purchase these items. Put the items in reusable totes or containers.

* * *

Can drive

Start an annual can drive for a charitable organization.

* * *

Meal Train Organizer

Help organize meal trains for new parents, the elderly, or people recovering from some debilitating illness or surgery. You can start by collecting the names of people that are interested in volunteering and helping your mission.

* * *

Gardening

Volunteer to work on an elderly neighbor's garden and yard. Is there anything prettier than a yard full of healthy, beautiful, bright colored flowers? Cheer up someone's day. The organization Little Brothers Friends of the Elderly's motto is "Flowers Before Bread". Offer your friendship and a beautiful garden to a lonely elder.

* * *

Be a friendly face at a nursing home.

Bring a basket of nail polish and remover to a nursing home. Offer to paint residents nails and have some friendly conversation. There are so many elderly residents that don't get regular visitors. You would be a very welcome face! The ladies will love the attention and the pretty nails.

* * *

BINGO!

Start a weekly BINGO party at an assisted living facility or in a nursing home community room. Bring small prizes such as; travel sized body lotion, playing cards, calendars, quarters, hair barrettes, books with large print, fun sunglasses, Hawaiian leis, window clings, hard candy (make sure to bring sugar free just in case someone is diabetic) small knickknacks that can be set in window sills or on night stands.

* * *

Start your own charity

Is there a charitable cause that you are absolutely passionate about? Start your own charity or foundation. It's definitely a great way to create a lasting legacy.

* * *

Raise a puppy for service

Raise a puppy for a service organization. There are many organizations for the blind, autism, and veterans that need puppy raisers. The organization provides compensation (e.g. vet visits, food) and you provide a loving environment. You could have the puppy anywhere from 6 months to 1 year. If you are an animal lover but also someone who desires to make a difference in someone's life, this would be something to look into.

* * *

Teacher's helper

Volunteer in elementary school classrooms. With budget cuts having an extra set of hands to staple papers together or type up announcements would be a huge help to teachers.

* * *

Angel Gowns

Start a collection for old wedding dresses and send them to an Angel Gowns program. The Angel Gowns program takes old wedding dresses and commissions seamstresses to transform the wedding dresses into beautiful burial gowns for newborn babies that pass away while their still in the hospital.

* * *

Brides Across America

Collect wedding dresses and donate them to Brides Across America. This is an organization Michelle Obama has commended. Wedding dresses are given to brides that are currently serving in the armed forces or their future spouses are serving in the armed forces. Money and logistics are very challenging for military couples, this is just one small thing that can be done to ease a little bit of stress.

* * *

Host a foreign exchange student

Host a foreign exchange student. It would be a unique opportunity to learn about another culture while also teaching someone about your own. If you have a spare room or an apartment-type space available this would be ideal for hosting a foreign student. Once you've been approved to host a student and you find out the student's information, make sure to do your research into where they are coming from. You could buy a book learning about their language and culture. Put up photographs or posters of things that will remind them of where they are coming from— make them feel more at ease and comfortable.

* * *

Home visitor

Become a home visitor for a hospice organization or an elderly visiting program (e.g. Little Brothers Friends of the Elderly).

Volunteer at a library to read during children's storytime.

Volunteer to walk dogs or play with cats at your local animal shelter.

Are you a member of a church? Check to see if there are volunteer opportunities or part-time office work available.

CHAPTER 6: Food, Fun and Games

Start a card or board game playing club

There are several easy card games to learn including Solitaire and Hearts. Board games such as Settlers of Cataan have really exponentially increased the popularity of board games in recent years. It's wonderful! Perhaps more and more people are needing a break from technology.

* * *

Host a weekly Friday movie night

In the warm, summer months and depending on your property you could host an outdoor movie night. All you would need is a film projector, which you can rent, and a very large white bed sheet to hang up from some place high—like the side of a house. Have people bring their own chairs and snacks. Kick back and enjoy the film!

* * *

Sell stuff you don't need or use anymore on Craigslist or eBay

This will provide you with some extra spending money. You can also resell stuff you find at yard sales or antique shops.

* * *

Refinish old thrift store finds

Chalk paint and shabby chic are extremely popular right now. You can find old desks, chairs, shelves for cheap or free on Craigslist or in your local newspaper.

* * *

Cookbook Author

Are people always asking for your potato coleslaw or chili recipe? Collect all of your treasured family recipes and put them together in a cookbook. You can then pass it out to family/friends for Christmas or birthdays.

* * *

Cooking Lessons

If you are a good cook, host your own cooking classes.

* * *

Road Trip

Make a list of all your childhood friends. Plan a road trip to visit all of them. See the sights while connecting with old friends. (Make sure to give them a few days notice!)

* * *

Visit Bed & Breakfasts and historic hotels all over different parts of the country.

Keep a journal recording your experiences and

take lots of pictures. You might even want to explore publishing your journal.

* * *

Join a book club

Check the bulletin board at your local library or bookstore for any announcements.

* * *

Join Goodreads

Sign up for a Goodreads account and put together a bucket list of books you want to read. Get recommendations from friends, read and write reviews, and discuss everything and anything related to books.

* * *

Join a fantasy sports league

Do you like statistics or probability? Join a fantasy sports league. You don't have to necessarily be a fan of a specific sports team, actually many of the top fantasy sports players aren't huge fans of sports—they're huge fans of statistics, sports theory, and psychology. It's an interesting, highly in-depth game of skill and chance. Of course there are also small fantasy games put together by friends and family that are great starting off points.

* * *

Learn a new game

Settlers of Cataan is an extremely popular board game. Become an 'expert' and start hosting games at your house or a local coffee shop.

* * *

Become a professional wedding crasher

Enjoy a weekend of silliness. Collect a couple of church bulletins or newspapers and find some interesting ones to attend! Keep a stash of wedding cards on hand. Don't forget to take a couple keepsake pictures in the photo booth.

* * *

Cook dinners for the homeless people in your area

Err on the side of caution and always have someone else go with you or at least know where you are going.

* * *

Shall we dance?

Take ballroom dance lessons. Have you ever seen the Richard Gere film *Shall We Dance?*—it's a great film about a middle-aged gentleman who pursues dance lessons and how his outlook on life changes as does his relationship with his wife.

* * *

Offer knitting classes at a local yarn store or library

You could either have students purchase the supplies and charge a nominal fee or offer the classes for free.

* * *

Chess Master

Learn chess! It's an easy game to learn but incredibly challenging to become good at.

* * *

Start a new tradition

Decorate trees for Valentine's Day or Easter! Buy a Christmas tree with the roots that you can replant it outside in your yard.

* * *

Meet the new neighbors

Host a neighborhood potluck or BBQ. People can get to meet anyone new that has moved into the neighborhood or get reacquainted with neighbors they haven't talked to in a while.

* * *

Selfies

Take a photograph of yourself every day in the same spot for a year or more.

* * *

Happy Thanksgiving!

Provide a needy family with a complete Thanksgiving dinner.

Christmas elf

Become a Christmas Elf and surprise a child or a family with a stocking full of presents. Choose a different family every year.

Help a child

Pick stars off the needy children Christmas tree.

Golfing

Learn how to golf. It's a great sport that all ages can play.

Antique Shop

Do you have an attic or garage filled to the brim with antiques you've collected over the years? Open up your own antique shop. You can do it right from your own home.

Pottery

Learn how to make pottery. Pottery classes are really popular right now and they're offered all across the country. There are make and take pottery stores as well.

* * *

Wine and cheese night

Have a bi-weekly wine and cheese night with friends.

* * *

Grape stomping

Have you seen the classic *I Love Lucy* episode where Lucy goes to Italy and somehow ends up stomping grapes with a feisty Italian woman? The scene ends with Lucy covered in grape juice! Plan a trip to stomp some grapes in Italy, and while you're there why not have a glass or 2 of wine!

* * *

Create a YouTube channel

Talk about makeup and beauty products or current events.

* * *

127 Corridor

Visit flea markets, specifically one called 127 Corridor. 127 Corridor is widely considered the World's Longest Flea Market. It begins in North Covington, Kentucky and ends in Gadsden, Alabama. This flea market will definitely take more than a day to go through but it will be worth it! It's a fantastic event that's held once a year in August. For 3-4 weeks over 2,000 vendors line a massive stretch of highway. If you love flea markets, 127 Corridor needs to go on your *must* do list.

* * *

Interviewer

Interview an elderly person with an interesting life story. Write their biography or craft a series of fictional stories based on their life experiences.

* * *

Learn to cook Indian food

Take Indian cooking lessons with your best friend.

* * *

Coffee lover

Become a coffee snob. Get to know a good cup of espresso from a bad one. Did you know the darker the coffee bean the less caffeinated it is? Learn this and more by reading about tasting different cups of coffee from around the world.

* * *

Review wine and/or beer

Start a blog reviewing all different types of wine or beer. Microbrews and select small batch wines are incredibly popular right now. You can slowly build up a following and you'll become known as an 'expert'. Businesses might even contact you to send you free products to try out and provide your honest review/feedback.

* * *

Organization expert

Do you love organization? Why not contact your local library and offer to teach a class on organizational skills.

* * *

The next Steven Spielberg?

Make a documentary. You don't need any fancy video equipment. Mobile phones do an amazing job of taking video. It can be on any subject that you are passionate about. If you need help overlaying any audio or perhaps creating graphics for an introduction turn to Fiverr.com to find some talented video editors or graphic designers. It will cost you as little as $5 to get work done. Make sure to read reviews for whoever you hire. Try a few different ones so that you get a variety of options to choose from.

* * *

Treasure Hunter

Geocaching. Have you heard of geocaching? Do you enjoy interactive games? Well you probably will like geocaching. Geocaching is a fun, recreational activity that involves tracking hidden items all around the world. It's real life treasure hunting game! All ages enjoy hunting for these hidden items by using GPS coordinates that are posted online. This treasure hunt is international and geocaching can be done in every country. Make sure to share photographs of your treasure online! Happy treasure hunting!

* * *

Mickey Mouse

Do you want to reconnect with your inner child? Let's head to Disney World! It's a magical destination for all ages—not just for children. Ride all the rides and attractions. Stuff yourself on all the treats—cotton candy, chocolate chip Mickey Mouse pancakes, funnel cake, and fried Twinkies (Yes, this is a real thing and yes, it is just as amazing as it sounds!)

* * *

Be on a game show

Try out for a game show! *Jeopardy, Wheel of Fortune, The Price is Right* are classic game shows that have designated tryout date/times. Check their websites or watch the shows end credits for information regarding upcoming tryouts. The important thing is to not give up! If you really want to be on the show, don't let the first rejection keep you from achieving your dream! Sometimes it has taken contestants dozens of tryouts. Also, tryout for a variety of game shows—not just one. Your chances of making it on a game show will be much higher. Before trying out for the show make sure you know all the rules and what the show is all about.

* * *

Invent the next best thing since sliced bread

Do you have an idea for a new product invention or something to improve an existing product?

Why don't you submit your idea through Edison Nation, an online hub for aspiring inventors to get together and create the next big thing! Think Snuggie or Eggies—both two huge As Seen on Television monster successes! Do you have the next Thighmaster idea scribbled in a sketchbook somewhere? There's a little Thomas Edison in all of us, let yours out to see the light of day.

* * *

Everyone loves handmade greeting cards

Create homemade greeting cards. Personalized and handmade items are highly sought after. When was the last time you received a handwritten greeting card in the mail? Chances are if it is someone's birthday that person will be receiving dozens of notifications on their cell phone that friends on Facebook have written 'Happy Birthday!' on their Facebook wall. Receiving a handwritten card, let alone a card without the Hallmark logo on the back, is something really special. The recipient's heart will warm into a giant puddle. You can create your own stash of homemade greeting cards for friends and family or expand your network and earn a little extra pocket money by selling your creations.

***

Give an inspirational talk

Have you ever watched a TED Talk? TED Talks are powerful talks given by people that simply have something to say that they believe will impact your life. There are TED Talks on everything under the sun, from how to sell a car to how to start thinking with a more positive frame of mind. Do you have something to talk about that you think would benefit someone else? Why don't you come up with a speech around 20 minutes in length that you would be comfortable speaking about to a room full of people.

***

Carpentry

Do you enjoy or have you ever been interested in woodworking? Well now is the time to either improve upon your skillset or just learn and build on a basic woodworking foundation. There are many places you can look to for guidance or lessons in woodworking. The easiest place to look is YouTube. There are thousands of wonderful tutorials for the beginner and the more seasoned professional alike.

***

Visit a saloon

Visit Deadwood, South Dakota. Make sure to really get into it and dress the part. Dress up like Calamity Jane or Wild Bill and have a whole lot of fun at the casinos and saloons!

***

Giddy-Up!

Take horseback riding lessons.

***

Search for Jimmy Hoffa

Search for Jimmy Hoffa. Supposedly after he left the parking lot of a restaurant in Bloomfield Township, Michigan, Jimmy Hoffa was never seen or heard from again. There have been many people to have claimed to know what happened to Hoffa but not one has ever panned out. Was he cremated and buried in the foundation of some new office building in downtown Detroit? Was his body cut up in pieces and fed to pigs? Maybe you can solve this infamous unsolved murder once and for all.

Take a ride

Ride a Harley-Davidson motorcycle across the desert.

* * *

Spontaneous Vacation

In the Jim Carrey film *Yes Man*, Carl Allen (played by Carrey) learns to say 'yes!' to every request. Carl and his girlfriend head to the airport and just ask the ticket agent to send them on whatever plane they can get on first. This leads to a whole lot of spontaneous fun in Lincoln, Nebraska. Make your next vacation a *Yes Man*-esque vacation and make it completely spontaneous. Have a blast going someplace you never would have thought of going.

* * *

Sturgic Motorcycle Rally

Go to the annual Sturgis Motorcycle Rally in South Dakota. It is a massive event held the first week in August. It was started in 1938 and is still going strong today. Even if you don't ride motorcycles it's still really incredible to see all the different bikes and there are plenty of events for you to partake in. It's also known as the Black Hills Motor Classic.

* * *

Host your very own scavenger hunt.

You can do this around a particular holiday or with a certain theme in mind. Invite friends and family to participate. You could even get small prizes to hand out to the winners. Be ready for some friendly competitive fun!

* * *

Experience a silent retreat

There are silent retreats offered by convents and religious centers across the world. They vary in length, the most popular retreat lengths are anywhere from 3-7 days. There are also silent retreats for those serious about delving deep into their faith or maybe they're interested in pursuing a career of religious service. It's a wonderful, indescribable feeling to be able to shut the noise of the world off and just be at one with yourself.

* * *

Woodstock. It's groovy, baby!

Woodstock is a music festival that started back in 1969 on a little dairy farm in New York State. The original event drew over 400,000 people! It was an iconic moment in music history for the 1960s. The event still continues to this day with bands like Graham Nash and the Allman Brothers.

* * *

Karaoke

Are you too afraid to get up on karaoke night at your favorite bar or restaurant? Well it's time to try out your singing voice. Don't be afraid to show off those pipes. Let loose and sing a song or two. Everyone is there for the same thing, to have a good time.

* * *

Start making Kombucha.

What's Kombucha? It's a very popular health drink that many claim to have healing properties. It's a fermented tea that has effervescence. When you initially taste it you might be put off by its strong vinegar taste. After a few sips you may really love it or you may really hate it. For some it's an acquired taste. You can make it at home fairly easily. There are many DIY instructions and tutorials available online. This drink first became popular when A-list celebrities like Madonna and Gwyneth Paltrow were spotted carrying bottles of Kombucha.

* * *

Spread laughter and joy

Enjoy comedy night, with you in the spotlight! Do your friends consider you the life of the party or do you have a really wicked dry sense of humor? If so, try your luck out on stage in front of an unbiased audience. Bring some of your best lines and a great attitude with you.

* * *

Crossfit

Have you always wanted to get in shape but just couldn't find the time or the will power and now you're nearing retirement age and you think it's too late to get in shape? Well, that is absolutely false. You can still get in the best shape of your life—yes, your life. Crossfit is a high-intensity workout program that's swept the country and some consider it a 'cult'. It's a fast workout that concentrates on functional movements and making you strong in the sense of using your body in the ways it was meant to be used and moved. People in their 70s have joined Crossfit and have seen tremendous results. All exercises have modifications. Certified coaches are there with you the whole time, walking you step-by-step through each workout of the day. (or as they call it "WOD") You definitely won't be bored, the workouts are different each day. There's no time to get bored! Another plus is the friendships you'll make! There are lots of positive attitudes and smiling faces cheering you on as you strive towards your goals.

* * *

Scrapbooking

Do you like art? Do you like scissors and stickers? As you go on your many trips and adventures as a newbie retiree, keep a page for each destination or person you encounter along your journey. There are fun stickers, miniature people, and all sorts of paper to be found at craft shops and specialty stores. This hobby will definitely be keeping you very busy. People that try it say they get sucked into it!

***

Make a quilt

Take old clothes that have meaning to them or that you just don't want to completely part ways with yet and make them into a beautiful quilt. If you don't know how to quilt, that's just one more thing you can learn!

***

Become a vegetarian or go completely vegan

Try it for several months and see how you feel. Do you have more energy? Are you finding yourself sick less often? If so, this lifestyle might be a good fit for you.

***

Time capsules

Create and bury time capsules. Include newspapers with the day's date, current music and movie selections, a mini biography, a menu from a popular restaurant, an old cell phone or television remote, and other interesting things that future generations will enjoy looking at. What would you enjoy seeing if you stumbled upon a time capsule from the early 1800s or even 1700s?

* * *

Find a BINGO hall and have some fun!

Find a random BINGO hall and play a few games. You might not win a million bucks but you might find you have some actual fun and meet some pretty interesting people. Just remember some of these BINGO halls have highly competitive people playing and they don't like being distracted with chit-chat. If you find yourself surrounded by non-chatty folks, just stick to yelling "BINGO!" and not much else.

* * *

Drive with the top down.

Rent or buy a convertible and drive up and down the coast of California or Route 66, which is also commonly referred to as America's 'Main Street'.

* * *

The Wrigley Mansion

Visit Lake Geneva, Wisconsin and see the Wrigley spearmint mansion. Stay at a B&B while you are enjoying your time in this quiet little elegant town that looks like it popped right out of the pages of a fairy tale or romance novel.

* * *

Pass it on

Perform 1,000 random acts of kindness and record them. Tell the people you are helping to 'pass it on'.

* * *

Dream house

Draw up plans for your dream house. How many

floors will it have? Will there be a fireplace in the master bedroom? What color will the guest room be? Have some fun perfecting your dream home. One day soon it could definitely become a reality.

* * *

Childhood games

Find someone to play double dutch with. It's an old classic game that you are sure to remember if you went to any primary school. Another fun classic is 'Red Rover, Red Rover' and then of course there's the old stand-by, hopscotch. Just remember you're not 8 years old on the school playground anymore so joints might creak a bit more with all the jumping and horsing around.

* * *

Be a political activist

Volunteer for a political party and pass of flyers or spread the word about the importance of voter registration. Check out your political party's website for more information and application instructions.

**

Home library

Create your own library. If you have hundreds or maybe even thousands of books sitting around, get them organized into genres. Invite friends and family over to check out books. This would be a great way to start off organizing a book club too. Each month present a new book that everyone should read and then discuss the book over coffee and cookies.

Final Words

The best part about retirement isn't necessarily having an abundance of leisure time, it's freedom! It's the freedom to not have to show up every single day at a 9-to-5 (unless you want to!). Enjoy this next chapter!

Retirement is all about "not living to work but working to enjoy living!" You have so many incredible opportunities to really do something exciting and fun ahead of you.

The only tough decision isn't what will you do but more along the lines of what won't you do! Chances are you have found several ideas that have already started the wheels spinning in your head.

Made in the USA
San Bernardino, CA
29 December 2016